D0119253

Eleanor Roosevelt

JUNIOR ▪ WORLD ▪ BIOGRAPHIES

Eleanor Roosevelt

JANE ANDERSON
VERCELLI

CHELSEA JUNIORS

a division of CHELSEA HOUSE PUBLISHERS

FRONTISPIECE: *Eleanor Roosevelt, age 21, in her wedding gown.*

English-language words that are italicized in the text can be found in the glossary at the back of the book.

Chelsea House Publishers

EDITORIAL DIRECTOR Richard Rennert
EXECUTIVE MANAGING EDITOR Karyn Gullen Browne
COPY CHIEF Robin James
PICTURE EDITOR Adrian G. Allen
ART DIRECTOR Robert Mitchell
MANUFACTURING DIRECTOR Gerald Levine

JUNIOR WORLD BIOGRAPHIES

SENIOR EDITOR Ann-Jeanette Campbell
SERIES DESIGN Marjorie Zaum

Staff for ELEANOR ROOSEVELT
EDITORIAL ASSISTANT Kelsey Goss
PICTURE RESEARCHER Villette Harris
COVER ILLUSTRATION Kye Carbone

Copyright © 1995 by Chelsea House Publishers, a division of Main Line Book Co. All rights reserved. Printed and bound in the United States of America.

First Printing

1 3 5 7 9 8 6 4 2

Library of Congress Cataloging-in-Publication Data
Vercelli, Jane Anderson.
    Eleanor Roosevelt / Jane Anderson Vercelli.
        p. cm.—(Junior world biographies)
    Includes bibliographical references and index.
    ISBN 0-7910-1772-9.
        0-7910-2136-X (pbk.)
    1. Roosevelt, Eleanor, 1884–1962—Juvenile literature. 2. Presidents' spouses—United States—Biography—Juvenile literature. [1. Roosevelt, Eleanor, 1884–1962. 2. First ladies.] I. Title. II. Series.
E807.1.R48V47 1994   94-5132
973.917'092—dc20   CIP
[B]   AC

Contents

*One of the triumphs of Eleanor's life was
the creation of the United Nations' Universal
Declaration of Human Rights.*

1

A Lifelong Career

On December 10, 1948, at 3:00 in the morning, the "hardest working delegate" to the United Nations (UN), Eleanor Roosevelt, experienced one of the greatest victories of her life. The General Assembly had just adopted the Universal Declaration of Human Rights, a "bill of rights" that would apply to the whole world. For two years Eleanor had chaired the 17-nation committee that drafted this important text. The assembly vote was 48 in favor, 2 absent, and 8 abstentions, but the delegation rose to its feet unanimously to give Roosevelt the ovation she deserved.

Eleanor's desire to recognize and protect the rights of humans everywhere began early in her life. Her most cherished teacher at boarding school, Marie Souvestre, was a strong believer in social justice. As a young woman, Eleanor had volunteered at a settlement house, teaching poor children dance and *calisthenics*. Even then she took her work seriously and was likely to choose going to the settlement house over going to a party.

In 1905, Eleanor married her distant cousin Franklin Delano Roosevelt, who would later become president of the United States. Marriage put an end to her volunteer work because as a new wife, Eleanor was expected to be absorbed in running a household and making a family. But Eleanor married into a household ruled by Franklin's dominating mother, Sara Delano Roosevelt.

More than anything, Eleanor wanted to be a good wife and daughter-in-law, but Sara put barriers in her way. Sara decided where the young couple would live, they all vacationed together at the Roosevelt house on the island of Campobello, and Sara stepped in to raise Eleanor's children. Eleanor was not happy about any of this, but her goal was to be dutiful, not happy.

Franklin Roosevelt was a sophisticated, good-looking young man-about-town. He had a taste for alcohol, parties, and adventures, which his wife did not share. Overshadowed by her mother-in-law and distanced from her children and husband, Eleanor fell into depression.

To counter her unhappiness, Eleanor decided she had to exert herself on behalf of her husband's career. "It was a wife's duty to be interested in whatever interested her husband, whether it was politics, books, or a dish for dinner," she explained.

Fortunately for Eleanor, in 1911, Franklin became a state representative in Albany, New York. Her wifely duty, therefore, was to be interested in politics, an area that suited her well. She became an enthusiastic supporter of her husband, the Democratic party, and, in particular, the reform movement that was trying to clean up politics and help the underprivileged. Her life became a whirlwind of meetings, luncheons, *lobbying* efforts, and simply getting to know who was who in the world of politics.

When Franklin was appointed assistant secretary to the navy in Washington, D.C., Eleanor left behind state politics and followed her newfound interests on the national level.

In 1917, when the United States entered World War I, Eleanor rediscovered her love of working for a good cause. She knitted for the troops, was a Red Cross volunteer, and fed soldiers passing through the nation's capital. Eleanor also visited sick, wounded, and shell-shocked soldiers. Outraged at the living conditions of the mentally ill war veterans, she successfully lobbied for federal funds to better their situation.

The end of the war in 1918 brought Eleanor's work to a halt, but not for long. The Russian Revolution had just put communism in place with promises of social reform. In the United States, unionizers were organizing factory workers and miners, and women were demanding and finally won the right to vote. Eleanor responded by becoming active in labor and political issues, particularly in the Women's Trade Union League and the League of Women Voters. She kept informed on legislation covering the rights of women and children, labor laws, and international peace, and she promoted progressive reform. While Eleanor worked for the rights of others, she also began to assert her own rights.

Eleanor took a stand against her mother-in-law's intrusions. She fired all the staff that her mother-in-law had hired for her Washington, D.C., house and replaced them with her own. Outside of the home, Eleanor met and worked with many new people, including a number of strong women activists who became her closest friends and members of her extended family.

Throughout the 1920s, Eleanor concentrated on forcing the Democratic party to listen to

In the 1920s, Eleanor made friends with other politically active women, such as Esther Lape (left), a prominent feminist.

its new constituency of voting women. She felt it was not enough to have the vote; women must have the power to set the agendas and call the shots, just as men did. To this end, she organized women, raised money, wrote articles and columns, edited the *Women's Democratic News,* and spoke to crowds and individuals. Eleanor Roosevelt was becoming a well-known name.

In 1921, Franklin's legs were left permanently paralyzed after an attack of *poliomyelitis,* or polio. While Eleanor felt that politics would help restore her husband, Sara urged him to retire from public life. This gave Eleanor three good reasons to step up her involvement in politics: her own satisfaction, Franklin's well-being, and the bedevilment of her mother-in-law's plans.

Franklin accepted the Democratic party's invitation to run for governor of New York in 1928. Wiping away any clouds of doubt over whether he was physically up to it, he simply did it, and won. Eleanor had not wanted him in the race. She was afraid that his return to public office would mean the end of her own political and private life.

It had been a long time since Eleanor had tried to make herself content with being only Franklin's wife. She had become an outspoken, independent thinker and activist, but she knew that the governor's wife would not have that freedom. She would have to be careful to do and say the "right" things and not to do and say the "wrong" things.

Three strands were woven together to save Eleanor from the life she dreaded: her marriage to Franklin had become a political partnership that gave them both security; she was living in an age when the roles of women were changing; and,

Eleanor posed for this portrait in 1932, when she was on the brink of becoming the nation's first lady.

finally, Eleanor had her own *indomitable* tempera-
ment. These elements helped her redefine the job
of a politician's wife.

As Eleanor went from being the first lady of
the state of New York to being the first lady of the
United States of America, the restrictions on her
grew. Her ability to dismiss them, however, grew
as well. Still, it was only after Franklin's death in
1945 that Eleanor was fully able to pursue her own
political career.

During holidays Eleanor traveled with her school's headmistress, who encouraged her to think independently and dress stylishly. This portrait was taken on a trip to Switzerland in 1900.

2

The Ugly Duckling

Anna Eleanor Roosevelt was born in New York City on October 11, 1884. Her parents—the wealthy and socially *prominent* Elliott and Anna Roosevelt—had been hoping their first child would be a boy. Instead, not only was she a girl, but some family members found her uglier and more wrinkled than most babies.

The upper-class society that Eleanor was born into consisted of a small group of wealthy families whose children grew up together and then married each other. When husbands and fathers worked, it was not out of necessity. Wives and mothers had children, ran households full of servants, and called on one another socially. A lot of customs, rules, and restrictions came with being in this class, and its members could be very unforgiving of behavior that was out of the ordinary.

Eleanor's father, Elliott, had two sisters and an older brother, Theodore "Teddy" Roosevelt, Jr., who would later become president of the United States. Elliott met Anna Hall, Eleanor's mother, in New York City. She was the beautiful daughter of a wealthy man. They were married on December 1, 1883. As prominent members of New York society, the couple lived richly and socialized with other such families. The social whirl, at least for Anna, ended when she became pregnant.

Elliott was not disappointed at all in the new baby. He was devoted to his daughter, his "miracle from heaven," with her luminous blue eyes and golden hair. But Anna thought young

Eleanor "old-fashioned," because she seemed so serious. Eleanor's father affectionately nicknamed her Little Nell; her mother teasingly called her Granny. Eleanor later recalled, "She often called me that for I was a solemn child, without beauty and painfully shy and I seemed like a little old woman entirely lacking in the spontaneous joy and mirth of youth."

When Eleanor was two-and-a-half years old, she and her parents and nurse set sail for

Anna Hall was considered one of the most beautiful women in New York society. When she was young, Eleanor was often unfavorably compared to her mother.

Europe on the *Britannic.* Out at sea on a foggy day, their ship was rammed by another. Luckily, the Roosevelts were not hurt, but Eleanor always remembered the "wild confusion" as she was handed over the side of the ship into the outstretched arms of her father, who was in a lifeboat. "I was terrified and shrieking, and clung to those

At age three, Little Nell, as Eleanor's father called her, already had the reputation of being a serious, shy child.

who were to drop me. Finally, I was safely in the little boat," Eleanor later related.

From then on, Eleanor was afraid of boats and of the sea. At various times in her life she was also scared of the dark, horses, dogs, and snakes. Years later, she said that she had a fear of "being scolded, afraid that other people would not like [her]."

Just before Eleanor's fifth birthday, her mother gave birth to a boy, Elliott junior. By then, Elliott senior was having serious problems with drinking. His alcoholism was making him thoughtless and cruel. He would disappear unexpectedly. A servant claimed he was the father of her child, and, eventually, his health began to decline.

Elliott's siblings, especially his brother, Teddy, forcefully joined the battle to set him right. All were concerned that Elliott's behavior would reflect badly on the rest of the family. The Roosevelts decided to take a long trip to Europe where Elliott would, they hoped, respond to cures.

In 1891, the family was living in a house outside Paris, France. Anna was pregnant again. Although Eleanor was only six years old, she was sent to a convent to get her out of the way of the new baby and her reckless father.

Eleanor was miserable. She pretended to swallow a penny in order to get attention. "I think it must have been evident that my story was not true, but I could not be shaken, so they sent for my mother and told her that they did not believe me. She took me away in disgrace."

When Eleanor left the convent, her new baby brother, Hall, was several weeks old. Elliott's behavior did not improve, and soon Eleanor's parents separated. Anna and the children returned to the United States.

Back in New York, Eleanor's mother became very ill with diphtheria, a contagious and, back then, usually a fatal disease. She died in 1892, only two years before a cure was found. Eight-year-old Eleanor and her brothers went to live with their grandmother Hall, who had no use for

Eleanor (right) sits with her father and her brothers,
Elliott junior (left) and Hall, in 1892. That year
Eleanor's mother and Elliott junior both died, and
her father continued to ruin himself with drink.

joy and laughter, and whose city house was dark
and grim. Only six months after Eleanor's mother
died, her brothers became ill with scarlet fever.
The baby, Hall, recovered, but Elliott junior devel-
oped diphtheria and died.

Eleanor's father was allowed to visit his children, but he could not live with them. When he visited, Eleanor was so happy that she slid down the banisters and "catapulted into his arms before his hat was hung up." Elliott's separation from his daughter was very painful for both of them.

Elliott wrote often to his Little Nell, who kept his letters all her life. In them, he suggested that they would have a life together one day. Eleanor treasured that dream. She did not see her father as the irresponsible *cad* everyone else saw. He was her hero.

Then, in the summer of 1894, when Eleanor was nine years old, her father suddenly died in the midst of a heavy drinking binge. Years later, Eleanor wrote that with her father's death, the hope for their future companionship died, "but he lived in my dreams and does to this day."

It seems that no one helped young Eleanor to understand what was happening to her and her family: the trauma of being sent away from her family to the convent, the separation from and then loss of her adoring father, the death of her brother, and the death of her mother, from whom she had never felt warmth.

For the next five years, Eleanor spent the winters in Grandmother Hall's house in New York City and the summers at Oak Terrace, her grandmother's country house in Tivoli, New York. Tall, thin, and shy, Eleanor was dressed by her grandmother in clothes ill suited to her size and age: dresses that were above the knee; long, black stockings, even in summer; and high-buttoned shoes that were supposed to keep her ankles slim. Eleanor's aunt Edith Roosevelt made a keen observation: "Poor little soul, she is very plain, but the ugly duckling may turn out to be a swan."

Eleanor had been schooled privately, with other girls from prominent families. At that time, education for girls was not considered important and most girls did not go to college. Eleanor was a good student who loved to read, but that was not why she was sent to boarding school. Grandmother Hall's two grown-up sons also had drink-

Marie Souvestre was much more to Eleanor than just a teacher. Eleanor's own love of teaching may have had its beginnings with their relationship.

ing problems. She felt that Eleanor would be better-off away from their bad influence.

Eleanor entered Allenswood, a girls' boarding school outside London, England, in 1899. The headmistress, Marie Souvestre—something of a free spirit—became the most important person in

Eleanor's life, second only to the memory of her father. Souvestre not only taught the standard courses but expected her students to ask questions and to think for themselves. She took a special interest in Eleanor's worldly education.

Souvestre and Eleanor traveled together during many holidays, with Eleanor responsible for all the travel arrangements. Souvestre encouraged her to experiment with grooming and fine clothing. They went to the theater, to visit friends, to museums and the like, but Souvestre also taught Eleanor how to change her plans in an instant, if she so desired.

Eleanor had to leave Allenswood to *come out* in New York society, but she kept the spirit and lessons of Marie Souvestre all her life. Before returning to New York in the early summer of 1902, Eleanor wrote, "I have spent three years here which have certainly been the happiest years of my life."

Eleanor and Franklin, here in Italy, toured Europe on their honeymoon. While in Scotland, Eleanor became aware of her ignorance of American government and vowed to educate herself.

3
Roosevelt
Weds
Roosevelt

In the summer of 1902, Eleanor was 17 years old. Electricity and gas stoves were replacing kerosene lamps and coal stoves. The Hall family was starting to use telephones and cars. Such modern conveniences brought revolutionary change, but New York society held on tightly to its age-old social customs, as Eleanor would discover.

Eleanor spent a lonely summer at Oak Terrace with a moody aunt and her uncle Vallie, who when drunk sometimes shot at people passing by his window. Understandably, Eleanor did not invite anyone to visit except her fifth cousin once removed, Franklin Delano Roosevelt. He was handsome, brimming with self-confidence, and already familiar with Vallie's oddities.

In the fall, Eleanor was to go through the ritual of coming out by attending large formal balls and dinners and smaller dances. At the invitation-only affairs, the young debutantes would be presented to the hostesses and asked to dance by the carefully selected young male guests. A primary purpose of coming out was to announce a girl's availability for marriage.

Debutantes were expected to do more than just attend parties. For instance, they were automatically listed as associate members of the Junior League, a women's organization dedicated to helping poor and unfortunate people. Few associate members ever actually volunteered for work, but Eleanor did. She taught dancing and calisthenics in a settlement house. In time she became a Junior League leader.

Eleanor and Franklin saw each other occasionally at dances, and one day, when Franklin was home from college, he went with her to visit one of her settlement-house students who was ill. After they left the child's impoverished home, Franklin took a deep breath of fresh air and said, "My God, I didn't know people lived like that."

The city slums were far removed from Springwood in Hyde Park, New York, the country estate where Franklin was born and raised. His mother, Sara Delano Roosevelt, was a strong-willed woman who had inherited more than a million dollars from her father. At the age of 26, Sara had married James Roosevelt, an older man with a son the same age as his new wife. Franklin was the only child they had together and they *doted* on him.

Franklin was educated at Groton, a private upper-class boys' school (he and Eleanor would send their four sons there), where his grade average was a C. He did not do well in sports but enjoyed performing in the choir, school plays, and debates.

In 1900, Franklin went to another prestigious school, Harvard University, in Cambridge, Massachusetts. That December, his father died and his mother rented an apartment near the university so she could be close to him. Three years later, Franklin invited Eleanor to the traditional

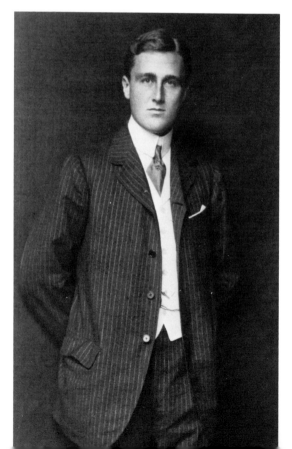

Franklin Delano Roosevelt was known for partying and flirting in his youth, but he went on to win four presidential elections, becoming the longest-serving president in U.S. history.

Harvard-Yale football game and proposed marriage to her. She accepted.

Franklin was 21 years old and Eleanor was 19. Their families had known each other since before the two were born. In fact, Eleanor's father, Elliott, had been Franklin's godfather.

Growing up, Eleanor had never really had a home she felt was her own. Her parents' troubles had kept the family moving, and then her mother's death and father's banishment had left her living in her grandmother's house. After boarding school, she was frequently sent to stay with various relatives. She looked forward to having her own home with Franklin, and to a close relationship with his mother.

When Franklin told his mother that he and Eleanor were engaged, she was surprised and upset. She had not wanted Franklin to marry so young. While Sara did not forbid the marriage, she persuaded Eleanor and Franklin to keep their engagement secret for a year.

Eleanor tried hard to express affection for Sara and to win her approval. In a letter to her future mother-in-law she wrote, "I do so want you to learn to love me a little. You must know that I will always try to do what you wish for I have grown to love you very dearly during the past summer." About Franklin she wrote, "I can only say that my one great wish is always to prove worthy of him."

Soon after Eleanor's 20th birthday, the couple's engagement was announced. The wedding date was set for March 17, 1905, St. Patrick's Day, and Eleanor's Uncle Teddy (President Theodore Roosevelt) would give the bride away.

Eleanor and Franklin received 340 wedding gifts, including many sets of books. Sara gave Eleanor a five-strand collar of pearls. Franklin gave her a gold watch pin with her initials in diamonds. Eleanor's wedding dress was satin and lace, with a long train. After the wedding, Uncle Teddy remarked, "Well, Franklin, there's nothing like keeping the name in the family."

While visiting friends in Scotland on their honeymoon, Eleanor was casually asked to explain the difference between national and state governments in the United States. She could not. "I had never realized that there were any differences to explain. In fact, I had never given a thought to the question," she later recalled. Right then she decided that she wanted to find out about the government under which she lived.

Franklin's mother Sara Delano Roosevelt (left) ruled the family. Eleanor energetically set about winning her over and spent years making the effort.

When the honeymooners returned to New York City, Sara had a house already rented and staffed for them. Eleanor had wanted to find her own home and hire her own help, but she was still eager to please her mother-in-law, so she did not complain. The two of them shared at least one meal every day, and Eleanor consulted Sara on all housekeeping details.

Eleanor and Franklin's first child, Anna Eleanor, was born on May 3, 1906. Ideas about raising children were different then. For example, doctors told mothers not to pick up their babies when they cried. Eleanor was advised that her infant needed lots of fresh air. To comply, Eleanor had a wooden basket built with *chicken wire* on the top and sides. She put her daughter in it and hung it out a bedroom window. Following the advice of her doctor, Eleanor paid no attention to her baby's cries. An outraged neighbor, however, threatened to report the Roosevelts to the Society for the Prevention of Cruelty to Children.

When Anna was born, Sara insisted that a nurse be hired for her. The following year, Eleanor gave birth to a son, James. She felt that she spent most of her early married life either pregnant or recovering from childbirth. Later, Eleanor wrote that if she had not had servants for the first few years, she would have gained more knowledge and self-confidence, and her children would have had happier childhoods.

Eleanor later said that her single worst mistake in life was having "too much belief in discipline when my children were young." Eleanor's daughter remembered that while her mother had felt a strong sense of duty to her children, she did not satisfy their need to feel close to her. Eleanor's mother had never been close to Eleanor, so perhaps she simply did not know how. Franklin, on the other hand, only wanted to have fun with his children. He could not bring himself to punish them, even when Eleanor insisted.

Every summer the family, including Sara,

traveled to Campobello, an island on the border of Maine and Canada, where Franklin's parents had built a vacation home. In 1908, their next-door neighbor died and in her will offered her house to Sara at a low price, if Sara bought it for Franklin's family. She did, and Eleanor finally had a house of her own. She filled it with wicker furniture and flowered wallpaper.

That same year, Sara bought land and had connecting houses built at 47 and 49 East 65th Street, in New York City: one for herself and one for Franklin and Eleanor. That autumn, Eleanor wept when she moved in. She again had to live in a house that was not hers. Perhaps worst of all, the two houses had sliding doors between them so Sara could come and go as she wished. Franklin told Eleanor she would feel differently in time. "I pulled myself together and realized that I was

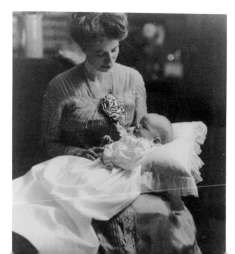

Anna Eleanor was born in 1906. Five sons would follow, one dying in infancy. It has been said that Franklin and Eleanor were better politicians than parents.

acting like a little fool, but there was a good deal of truth in [my feelings], for I was not developing any individual taste or initiative."

Eleanor's third child, Franklin junior, born on March 18, 1909, was "the biggest and most beautiful of all the babies." But that autumn, he became ill and died. Many children in the early 20th century did not live to adulthood, but that did not lessen Eleanor's grief.

Early in 1910, Franklin, then working as a law clerk, was asked to consider running as a Democratic candidate for the state senate in New York. "I doubt if anyone thought he had a chance," Eleanor said, but Franklin was enthusiastic and he won.

Franklin was a Democrat, but he hoped to pattern his political career after his famous Republican uncle, the former U.S. president Theodore Roosevelt: first, state legislator; second, assistant secretary of the navy; third, governor of New York; and finally, president of the United States.

Louis Howe (far left) was one of the most important members of the Roosevelts' extended family. He struck some people as repulsive, some as a political genius, and others as both.

4

A New Partnership

When Eleanor and Franklin moved to Albany, New York, Eleanor was free of Sara's daily influence for the very first time. Eleanor followed the example of her aunt Bye, Uncle Teddy's sister, whose house, nicknamed the Little White House, had been a Washington, D.C., center for intellectuals and politicians. Under Eleanor's care, their family home in Albany also became a popular place where politicians met to talk informally.

Eleanor began to be personally and politically active. She learned a great deal about the craft and substance of politics from listening to the Albany politicians talk in the evening, and she loved meeting and talking with them and their wives. She attended debates in the state house and discovered that she felt strongly about labor and government reform.

People were attracted to Eleanor and listened to what she had to say. Franklin increasingly sought her political advice and insight, which in the years to come would become a foundation of their marriage.

Perhaps the most important event to take place in Albany occurred when the Roosevelts met Louis Howe, a controversial newspaper reporter and political genius. Howe later became a very close member of their extended family, and he was later credited with making Franklin the president of the United States.

In 1913, Franklin was appointed assistant secretary of the navy in President Woodrow

Wilson's administration, and, accompanied by Howe, the family moved to Washington, D.C. There, wives of administration officials spent their afternoons calling at one another's houses. They spent their evenings at banquets or receptions or dining out. Eleanor needed a secretary to keep track of her appointments and to handle her mail. She hired 22-year-old Lucy Mercer, who had blue eyes, gracious manners, and a pleasing personality.

In 1914, the second Franklin junior was born on August 17. John, the youngest, was born on March 13, 1916. With America's entry into World War I in the spring of 1917, Eleanor's roles as wife, mother, and political adviser expanded to include war volunteer work. The war years would change her life.

Franklin returned from a battlefront tour of Europe in 1918 so ill with double pneumonia that he had to be carried off his ship on a stretcher. When Eleanor unpacked his luggage she found love letters from her secretary, Lucy Mercer, to

Franklin. Eleanor was shocked. She later said, "The bottom dropped out of my own particular world, and I faced myself, my surroundings, my world, honestly for the first time."

The reactions in the immediate family were swift and firm. Eleanor offered Franklin a divorce, but his mother said that if he left his wife and five children, she would no longer help him financially

Five years after hiring Lucy Mercer as a secretary, Eleanor discovered love letters from her to Franklin.

and he would not inherit the family house at Hyde Park. Howe told Franklin a divorce would ruin his political future.

Their son James later wrote that his parents "agreed to go on for the sake of appearances, the children and the future, but as business partners, not as husband and wife, provided he end his affair with Lucy at once, which he did. After that, Father and Mother had an armed truce that endured to the day he died." In 1920, Lucy married a wealthy widower, but she kept in touch with Franklin.

It would take Eleanor the next few years to recover from this betrayal. For some time she could not eat and she could not look anyone in the eye. But now she felt free to pursue her own interests and, in the end, make her marriage an equal partnership.

There was political as well as personal upheaval in the air. During the postwar anti-Communist activity called the Red Scare, Eleanor and Franklin came home one night to find that the nearby house of a Red Scare leader had been

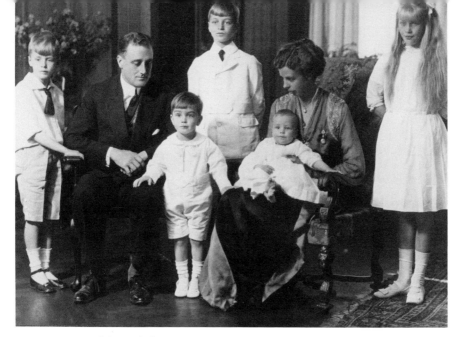

Although her marriage was shattered, Eleanor's sense of duty and loyalty helped keep the family together.

bombed, killing the bomb-throwing terrorist. Eleven-year-old James had been awakened by the commotion. "What are you doing out of bed at this hour, James?" Eleanor greeted him. "It's just a little bomb!" Those words became a family joke. In moments of excitement someone was likely to say, "It's just a little bomb!"

The Democratic National Convention in 1920 nominated Franklin for vice-president on a ticket with James M. Cox for president. Eleanor was uneasy about Franklin running for national office but was enthusiastic about the possibility of the League of Nations, the forerunner of the United Nations, becoming part of the Democratic platform. In an interview, she chose to focus on that rather than appear *ambivalent* over her husband's nomination: "I am particularly interested in the League of Nations issue. . . . We fought for it, and we should adopt it."

The 1920 campaign gave Franklin national exposure with a number of whistle-stop railroad tours across the country. When the train stopped, he would get off or stand on a balcony at the back of the caboose and give speeches, shake hands, and kiss babies.

Howe was there writing speeches, finalizing schedules, meeting people, and managing Franklin. Eleanor was there, too. Franklin wanted her to clip newspaper articles and keep notes about the trip. Franklin's image was helped when his wife stood beside him as he spoke or greeted people. When he was not in the public eye, however, Franklin was usually playing poker with his pals. Eleanor spent most of her time alone in her train compartment, reading or knitting.

Howe started his own campaign to win over Eleanor, asking her opinion of Franklin's speeches and press conferences. Soon they were talking for hours. Then others joined them. Eleanor felt that her ideas and the way she expressed them were valued; her input was important.

When Eleanor had first met Howe, she had not liked him. He smoked nonstop and was careless about his appearance and cleanliness. Some people found Howe downright repulsive in person. By the end of the 1920 campaign, however, he and Eleanor were close friends. According to Eleanor's cousin Corinne Alsop, it was Howe who inspired Eleanor to look outside of her traditional role as a wife and mother to find her place as a great world figure.

Republican candidate Warren G. Harding won the election, and the Roosevelts moved back to New York where Franklin joined a law firm.

Marguerite "Missy" LeHand, who had worked at Democratic headquarters, went to work as Franklin's secretary and became another loyal member of the Roosevelt family.

The following summer, Franklin was stricken with polio while vacationing with the family on Campobello. At first he felt tired and cold. He ran a high fever and lost the use of his legs. The rest of his limbs were very weak. His skin became so sensitive that even his bedsheets caused him pain. Eleanor nursed him day and night,

In his first national campaign, Franklin ran as the vice-presidential candidate alongside James M. Cox (left) for president. They lost.

taking turns with Howe, who by now had permanently moved into the Roosevelt house. Franklin spent six weeks recovering in New York City, but his life and Eleanor's would never be the same.

Eleanor described the stressful winter of 1921–22 as the hardest of her life. She and Howe wanted Franklin to pursue his political career. Sara wanted her son to retire from public life and live at Hyde Park. Franklin wanted to walk again.

To keep Franklin in touch with politics, Howe suggested that Eleanor "do some political work" of her own. At first she could think of nothing to do, but then she looked around her and found several issues that she felt strongly about.

It had become obvious in the 1920 campaign and election that while women had won the right to vote, they had not yet gained the power to influence the issues. Eleanor became involved in both the *bipartisan* League of Women Voters and the Democratic party in New York, fighting for women's rights, workers' rights, and the League of Nations.

Eleanor became good friends with seasoned feminists Elizabeth Read and Esther Lape and spent many enjoyable hours in their Greenwich Village apartment. Greenwich Village, a part of New York City, was home to many radical and artistic people: writers, politicians, artists, and feminists. New York high society would have been shocked that Eleanor spent her time there.

In the end, Franklin left public life for seven years. Eleanor and Howe kept him engaged in politics by being active in it themselves and bringing their friends and colleagues to visit him. Howe encouraged him to write letters to politicians on a variety of subjects, and he coached Eleanor in public speaking so that by giving talks, she would help keep the Roosevelt name alive. It was as much her own name as her husband's, however, that she kept before the public eye.

A close friend of Eleanor's later wrote honestly about her speaking abilities: "She was not a good speaker. Her voice, normally soft and pleasant, would become shrill when she was making speeches. She also had a nervous habit of laughing when there wasn't anything to laugh at." Eleanor usually spoke without a prepared speech and she peppered her talks with overly modest phrases such as, "I don't know, but . . ."

In 1922, the Democratic State Committee's women's division needed a famous speaker for a luncheon. Eleanor was called and agreed to appear. There she first met two of her closest friends.

Nancy Cook, a lawyer, and Marion Dickerman, a teacher, shared a Greenwich Village apartment. Together with Eleanor they bought the Todhunter School for Girls in Manhattan. Eleanor taught American history, current events, and

Eleanor (fourth from right) and friend Nancy Cook (far right) enjoy an outing with their students from the Todhunter School for Girls in New York City.

English and found that she loved teaching. It recalled her own exciting years at school with her beloved teacher, Marie Souvestre.

Cook and Dickerman quickly became members of the extended Roosevelt family. On the Hyde Park estate, but several miles from Sara's house, Franklin took charge of building a stone cottage called ValKill as a refuge for Cook, Dickerman, and Eleanor.

There the three women set up a furniture factory. Cook in particular had a talent for woodworking, but while the furniture was beautifully made, the factory was a financial failure. ValKill, however, was more than just a factory to Eleanor and her friends. It was a home where they made the rules, where women were not second-class citizens, and where they could enjoy each other's company.

By April 1928, when Eleanor published an article called "Women Must Learn To Play the Game as Men Do," the feminist hopes of the early

1920s had dimmed a little. "Women have been voting for ten years," she wrote. "But have they achieved actual political equality with men? No. . . . In small things they are listened to; but when it comes to asking for important things they generally find they are up against a blank wall."

In 1928, Franklin was elected governor of New York. By then, Eleanor was a well-known, forceful figure in politics and women's rights. She chaired committees, funded and supported many causes, spoke frequently, and wrote in popular magazines and newspapers. She had even been arrested for disorderly conduct at a demonstration supporting workers on strike.

Becoming the first lady of New York frustrated Eleanor. To what extent could she remain an independent activist, and to what extent would she have to retire behind the scenes as the governor's wife? She refused to give up her teaching at the Todhunter School, which meant spending many days a week away from home. At the same time, she did not show a shred of jealousy when

Franklin's secretary took over the first lady's duties in her absence.

As the governor's wife, Eleanor shaped a role for herself that she continued to fill when she became the nation's first lady. She was Franklin's legs, eyes, and ears, going places it was difficult for him to go and reporting back to him. She also made *astute* political suggestions, often bringing his attention to matters of importance to women, reminding him of his constituency of women, and recommending individual women for political appointments.

Personally, Eleanor and Franklin were busy building their new partnership. They relied on each other for support, and they influenced each other's ideas and actions. Neither looked to the other for romance in their marriage anymore, but they were fiercely loyal to each other and presented a united front. This strong union would last until Franklin's death in 1945.

Eleanor changed the role of the nation's first lady from hostess to activist. Here in 1935 she went underground to see firsthand the working conditions of miners.

5

"Plain, Ordinary Mrs. Roosevelt"

In November 1932, Franklin was elected president of the United States. During his campaign, Eleanor had continued to fulfill her own commitments rather than accompany him on the campaign trail. She paid close attention, however, not to publicly disagree with Franklin on any issues. While they both held progressive ideas on labor rights, education, general welfare, and women's issues, they also had their differences. When they did, Eleanor felt it was her responsibility to keep quiet.

Eleanor was happy for her husband, but not for herself: "This meant the end of any personal life of my own." Eleanor would now have to give up teaching, which she loved. Inside, Eleanor wanted simply to refuse to be the first lady; she was "just going to be plain, ordinary Mrs. Roosevelt. And that's all." But Franklin was reelected in 1936, 1940, and 1944, so Eleanor had little choice but to completely redefine the job of first lady to suit her.

Eleanor was concerned that her life would have to conform to tradition and *propriety* when she became the nation's first lady. But as soon as Franklin won the election, Eleanor set about doing things her own way. She argued against having Secret Service protection, even though she was without her own private bodyguard, Earl Miller, for the first time since 1929. Waving aside the traditional government car and military escort, she walked to her first White House visit with her new friend, Lorena Hickok.

Miller had been Eleanor's bodyguard and very close friend for years. An athletic man—once a circus acrobat—Miller encouraged Eleanor to enjoy herself playing tennis, horseback riding, swimming, even practice shooting. They were obviously very fond of each other and were considered virtually inseparable. But when the Roosevelts moved to Washington, D.C., Miller did not go with the extended family, which included Missy LeHand and Louis Howe. He stayed in New York and went to work in the Department of Corrections.

Fortunately for Eleanor, she met Lorena Hickok. Hickok was one of the very few female news reporters at the time, and the first to be assigned to cover a first lady. She and Eleanor hit it off immediately. Hickok inspired the idea that Eleanor should give press conferences and only invite women reporters. This was another departure from the traditionally quiet role of first lady, and it was successful.

Women press reporters scooped their male counterparts when Eleanor (seated, center) established her weekly press conferences for women only.

The entire country seemed to need something new, for when Franklin took office in 1933, the Great Depression was in full swing. Banks were failing and people could not find jobs. At his inauguration, Franklin spoke his famous words to a country in panic: "The only thing we have to fear is fear itself."

During the Roosevelt years, the government took new responsibility for its people, especially in

60

employment and housing. Congress passed many New Deal reform bills to provide relief for the poor and create jobs for the unemployed. Programs were started to set up Social Security for the elderly, oversee wages and work hours, provide electricity for communities, build highways, create art and literature, and more.

These were issues Eleanor cared about. But she was worried that she would be a prisoner in the White House, only allowed to be a hostess, stand in receiving lines, and organize official events. In 1939, there were 323 house guests at the White House, and 4,729 people came to a meal, 9,211 people came to tea, and 14,056 people came to receptions. At one event, Eleanor shook the

In September 1935, Eleanor greets the president's audience from the back of a train in Fremont, Nebraska.

hands of 3,100 guests in an hour and a half. But she still managed to remain politically active.

As in New York, Eleanor was once again Franklin's field reporter and roving ambassador at home and abroad. She visited Washington, D.C.'s back alleys, which were teeming with disease and crime. She went to Appalachia and talked with families of coal miners—and successfully organized the governmental effort to build affordable housing for them. (She privately funded a hospital there as well.) During World War II, she even toured the Pacific front.

Eleanor answered letters and wrote articles. In 1936, she launched her "My Day" daily newspaper column. During her first year in the White House, she received 300,000 pieces of mail. She came to realize that the people in the receiving lines, the people she met on the road, and the people who read her column in the newspaper saw her as a symbol linking them to their government.

Perhaps Eleanor is most widely remembered for her support of singer Marian Anderson.

In 1939, the Daughters of the American Revolution, a club to which Eleanor belonged, refused to allow Anderson to sing at Constitution Hall because she was black. The first lady promptly resigned her membership.

Anderson did sing, though not at Constitution Hall. Invited by the secretary of the interior (at Eleanor's suggestion) on Easter Sunday, 1939, Anderson gave an electrifying concert on the steps of the Lincoln Memorial, singing to an audience of 75,000 people.

The first lady supported black civil rights on a more basic level, too. One of the most *heinous* crimes committed against blacks was lynching. Blacks suspected or charged with breaking the law, or even simply upsetting the *status quo,* would be executed by whites, and they were sometimes tortured and mutilated before or after death. Frequently, lynching was merely an outlet for racial hatred. Usually the whites who committed lynchings went unpunished. Eleanor lobbied Congress to pass an antilynching bill. She convinced

After the DAR barred singer Marian Anderson from Constitution Hall, Eleanor helped arrange this historic performance, when Anderson sang from the steps of the Lincoln Memorial for a crowd of 75,000 on April 9, 1939.

Franklin to support it, but he was concerned that it would upset some of his political allies who saw nothing wrong with lynching. An antilynching bill was never passed.

Eleanor and Franklin seemed more successful as politicians than they were as parents. While Eleanor loved "all mankind," that left little room for her children. And if they wanted to see their father privately, they had to make an appointment. When the Roosevelt children had problems, they handled them alone or consulted their grandmother.

At 86 years of age, however, Sara Roosevelt was quite an old woman. When Eleanor saw her at Hyde Park in July 1941, her appearance was alarmingly frail. Eleanor urged Franklin to visit her as soon as possible. He did not arrive until September 6, when son and mother spent the day talking of old times. That night Sara lapsed into a coma, and the next day she died. Oddly, within minutes of Sara's death, one of the largest oak trees at Hyde Park crashed to the ground—and there had not been a breath of wind.

There was more disaster to come. On December 7, 1941, the Japanese attacked Pearl Harbor, and the United States entered World War II. All four Roosevelt boys served in the United States Armed Forces, and all returned home safely. Eleanor herself traveled far and wide, visiting American soldiers.

In 1944, Franklin won a fourth term as president. He had guided the country through the Great Depression and he wanted to see it through World War II. In March 1945, he went to his cottage in Warm Springs, Georgia. There, on April 12, as he was sitting for his portrait he got a terrible headache. He slumped over and died of a broken blood vessel in the brain. Lucy Mercer was with him.

It disturbed Eleanor that her old rival Lucy Mercer entered her life again at this point. Mercer and Franklin had seen each other from time to time

Franklin and Eleanor during the 1941 presidential inauguration. After 12 years in the White House, it took Eleanor only 12 days to move out after Franklin's death.

over the years, and Eleanor's daughter, Anna, knew of Mercer's presence in Warm Springs, but she had not told her mother. Eleanor had weathered Franklin's affair with Mercer in 1918; from then on, she had relied on Franklin as a partner. She would not have been hurt romantically, but she could still have felt betrayed.

In Washington, D.C., Eleanor said, "I am more sorry for the people of this country and of the world than I am for ourselves." Franklin's body was buried in Sara's rose garden.

Less than a month later, Germany surrendered. Later in 1945, Harry S. Truman, who followed Franklin as president, gave the order for two atomic bombs to be dropped on Hiroshima and Nagasaki, in Japan. Japan surrendered. The *Allies* had won World War II.

Within 12 days of Franklin's death, Eleanor had moved out of the White House and returned to New York, saying, "The story is over." But she was wrong.

At the UN, Eleanor proved herself an able diplomat and stateswoman in the service of justice and peace. Here she listens to a simultaneous translation of a UN delegate's speech.

6

First Lady
of the World

After Eleanor left the White House, she and her secretary of 30 years, Malvina "Tommy" Thompson, established their home base at ValKill. (Eleanor claimed that only with Tommy's death in 1953 did she understand for the first time what it was like to be alone.)

From 1945 until her death in 1962, Eleanor was free from the burden of being a politician's wife. For the first time, she could speak out, even controversially, and not worry about anyone's career but her own.

It was, however, unclear just what Eleanor would do with herself now that she was on her own. There was talk about her running for public office, even for president, but she refused. She recognized that women in politics had yet to gain real power, so she felt she could reach a much wider audience as a private citizen. Also, as Marie Souvestre had taught her and as she herself had taught at Todhunter, Eleanor believed that citizens as well as public officials should take social responsibility on themselves.

One cause above all others ignited Eleanor during the years of World War II and its aftermath: the formation of the United Nations (UN). When the horrors of the war became known, a worldwide appeal for peace was raised. Many, including Eleanor, felt that the only chance for peace was the UN, an institution that was meant to solve international problems without going to war.

President Truman, who called her the First Lady of the World, appointed Eleanor to the American delegation attending the first meeting of the UN General Assembly in 1946. The delegation assigned Eleanor to work on the committee devoted to human rights and cultural affairs.

This assignment fit Eleanor's theory about women and power. Committee 3, as it was called, was not expected to be important—just right for a middle-aged president's widow. Little did anyone suspect that human rights would become one of the most important issues of the 20th century and that Eleanor was no average middle-aged president's widow.

Eleanor's first battle at the UN was over the issue of political *refugees*. The Russians believed that how they treated political refugees was a private matter, no business of the UN's. Eleanor led the opposition and won, first in the committee, then in the General Assembly, where she *sparred* with the Soviet Union's premier debater.

This experience convinced Eleanor all the more that American democracy had to win over Soviet communism in the *cold war*. It also gained her widespread respect at the UN, where her next task was to chair the committee charged with writing a universal declaration of human rights.

The task of getting more than a dozen representatives from different countries to agree on the basic rights of all men and women fell to Eleanor. The Chinese insisted that the declaration include eastern philosophy. Women from India explained that if the word "men" was used to represent both men and women, in their country it would still mean only men. Communism and democracy battled over issues of society and individuality. There were seemingly endless stages of approval. The declaration finally did pass, however, and became one of the preeminent documents of the century.

The creation of the state of Israel and its status in the UN took precedence next. After World War II, many thought that there should be a Jewish state where war refugees and others could rebuild their lives. Some felt that countries such as Palestine and the United States should take in the refugees as immigrants. After much debate, stalling, and political maneuvering, Israel was formed and was admitted as a member of the UN in 1949.

At one point, however, Eleanor was so upset by the United States's unreliable behavior on this issue that she tried to resign. She felt the United States no longer supported the UN. President Truman rushed to assure her that the United States did support the UN and that she herself was far too important to her country, to the UN, and to the world to even think of resigning.

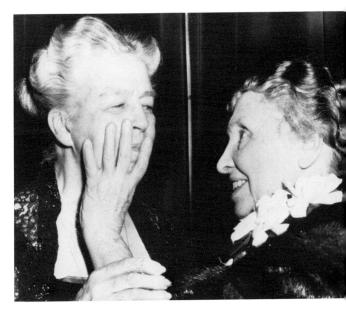

Dr. Helen Keller, shown here reading Eleanor's lips, was impressed by the Universal Declaration of Human Rights: "My soul stood erect, exultant, envisioning a new world where the light of justice for every individual will be unclouded."

At the end of 1952, Eleanor did resign from the U.S. delegation to the United Nations. Republican general Dwight D. Eisenhower had won the presidential election, and as a courtesy Eleanor offered to step down because he might want a Republican in her place. Many did not think the new president would dare replace the First Lady of the World, even though they held different political views, but he did.

Not long after, Eleanor showed up in the offices of the American Association for the United Nations (AAUN) asking if they could use her as a volunteer. They were *flabbergasted*. They did not have an available office to give her, but she assured them that she would be fine in a small cubicle. She wanted to build *grassroots* support for the UN and to educate people about what the UN stood for and what it could do to preserve peace.

While at the UN, Eleanor continued her other work. She kept up with her writing, which by now also included her autobiography. She joined the governing boards of the AAUN and of

Brandeis University, where she also lectured. She promoted the work of many interest groups, including the United Jewish Appeal and the National Association for the Advancement of Colored People (NAACP). On top of all this, she frequently attended, hosted, and spoke at special occasions and ceremonies. Many people felt Eleanor went too far, however, when she began to do television commercials and host radio and television talk shows.

Eleanor traveled more than ever. She had gained so much respect as the wife of a beloved president and as a world leader herself that on her visits abroad she was frequently treated as if she were an official of the United States government. She met royalty and heads of state; attended receptions, memorials, and military reviews; toured hospitals, schools, and slums; made speeches and held press conferences; and smiled and shook hands all around the world.

The 1950s brought to the forefront an issue that had haunted Eleanor throughout most of her

*In 1957, Eleanor met with Soviet leader Nikita
Khrushchev in the Soviet Union. When she was
criticized for socializing with the Communist leader,
she responded, "if we are going to live together we
have to talk."*

adult life: that one could be prohibited from saying
what one thought or from joining activities one
valued. The cold war was raging to prove which
was better: democracy or communism. To many
Americans, communism became a frightening
word, and they began to suspect people of hiding
the fact that they were really Communists.

Senator Joseph McCarthy of Wisconsin
started a campaign to discover who these people
were. He headed the House Committee on Un-
American Activities, which called many people to
testify about themselves or people they knew. The
hearings are famous for the damage they did to

individual careers and to the government's reputation. They also stand as a lesson in fanaticism and paranoia.

A number of Eleanor's friends and colleagues—including people associated with the UN—were suspected, and some were called before McCarthy's committee. One of Eleanor's longtime enemies declared that she should defend herself before McCarthy, but the House committee backed down. Eleanor hastened to reconfirm her basic civil liberties: "I want to be able to sit down with anyone who may have a new idea and not be afraid of contamination by association. In a democracy you must be able to meet with people and argue your point of view—people whom you have not screened beforehand. That must be part of the freedom of people in the United States."

In 1960, future president John F. Kennedy specially requested a meeting with Eleanor. It seemed that the blessing of the Democratic party's matriarch was what he wanted. She thought he would make a good president but that he was not appointing enough women to positions of power in the government. She promptly supplied him with a long list of women who she thought were qualified.

In 1962, Eleanor became ill and was hospitalized in September with tuberculosis of the bone marrow. The last days of her life were frustrating, according to her biographer Joseph P. Lash. She knew she was dying, but the doctors and nurses kept trying more tests and more treatments that would keep her alive. All her life people wanted from her something other than what she had to give and she had to teach them to accept who she was. Now she angrily struggled to teach the people who wanted her to live that she was ready to die.

On November 7, 1962, Anna Eleanor Roosevelt, aged 78, died. It was her wish to be buried in a plain wooden coffin covered with pine branches from the woods around ValKill. Her grave is next to Franklin's. Among the mourners at her funeral were former president and first lady

Harry and Bess Truman; former president Dwight D. Eisenhower; current presidential couple John F. and Jacqueline Kennedy; and future president and first lady Lyndon B. and Lady Bird Johnson.

Eleanor Roosevelt was born in one century and helped to change the course of another. She redefined herself personally, changing from society debutante to political wife, and reshaped the role of the first lady to include civic activism.

After Franklin's death, she spread her wings and took off as a worldwide champion of human rights. Remembered by poet Archibald MacLeish, she was "a woman who stood for compassion and hope in every continent of the earth—for courage and for belief."

By 1960, Eleanor, the grande dame of the Democratic party, had become a living symbol of dedication, social justice, individual responsibility, and progress.

CRATIC NATIONAL CO
1960

Further Reading

Freedman, Russell. *Eleanor Roosevelt.* New York: Clarion, 1993.

Lash, Joseph P. *Life Is Meant To Be Lived.* New York: Norton, 1984.

McAuley, Karen. *Eleanor Roosevelt.* New York: Chelsea House, 1987.

Roosevelt, Eleanor. *This I Remember.* New York: Harper and Brothers, 1949.

———. *This Is My Story.* New York and London: Harper and Brothers, 1937.

———. *You Learn By Living.* Philadelphia: The Westminster Press, 1960.

Sadler, Christine. *America's First Ladies.* New York: Macfadden-Bartell Corporation, 1963.

Toor, Rachel. *Eleanor Roosevelt.* New York: Chelsea House, 1989.

Glossary

Allies   referring to the nations united against Germany, Italy, and Japan in World War II or those united against the Central European powers in World War I

ambivalent   having conflicting attitudes or feelings at the same time; being uncertain

astute   keenly clever and aware

bipartisan   involving members of two political parties

cad   one who shows a shocking disrespect for good taste and has a disregard for others

calisthenics   rhythmic body exercises

chicken wire   a light wire netting

cold war   a conflict between the United States and the Soviet Union over whether democracy or communism should be the world's primary form of government

come out   to emerge into public view and be introduced as a respected member of upper-class society; generally refers to a teenage girl's debut

dote   to treat with excessive fondness or attention

flabbergasted   overwhelmed with shock or surprise

grassroots   relating to society at the local levels, from the ground up

heinous   hatefully or startlingly evil

indomitable   incapable of being controlled

lobby   to try to influence legislators and public officials through various organized activities

poliomyelitis   a contagious virus disease that can cause paralysis, and often leads to permanent disability

prominent   widely and popularly known

propriety   the quality of conforming to what is socially accepted

refugee   a person who flees to a foreign country to escape danger or suffering

spar   to engage in a dispute, trading arguments back and forth

status quo   the existing state of affairs in a society

Chronology

1884   Born Anna Eleanor Roosevelt on October 11 in New York City

1892   Deaths of Eleanor's mother, Anna Hall Roosevelt, and her brother, Elliott junior

1894   Eleanor's father, Elliott senior, dies

1899   Eleanor attends Allenswood, a girls' boarding school in England

1905   Marries Franklin Delano Roosevelt, a distant cousin, on March 17

1906   The couple's first child, Anna Eleanor, is born; over the next 10 years, five more children follow

1909   The first Franklin junior is born on March 18, but dies later that year

1910   Franklin wins a seat in New York State senate; the Roosevelts move to Albany

1913   Franklin named assistant secretary of the navy; family moves to Washington, D.C.

1917   The United States enters World War I;
Eleanor becomes a volunteer for the
war effort

1918   Eleanor discovers her secretary's love
letters to Franklin

1920   Eleanor joins the League of Women
Voters; Franklin loses vice-presidential
campaign

1921   Franklin contracts polio, which leaves
him crippled

1927   With her friends, Eleanor buys Todhunter School, and begins teaching there

1928   Franklin is elected governor of New
York; Eleanor acts as his field reporter
and political counselor

1932   Franklin is elected president of the
United States; Eleanor works for the
rights of women and minorities, anti-
poverty programs, and world peace

1936   Begins publishing her daily newspaper
column, "My Day"

1939   Resigns her membership to the Daughters of the American Revolution over racial discrimination against singer Marian Anderson; Anderson performs on the steps of the Lincoln Memorial on April 9

1941   The United States enters World War II

1945   Franklin dies on April 12; Eleanor moves to ValKill

1946   Eleanor is appointed to the committee devoted to human rights and cultural affairs at the UN General Assembly

1948   The General Assembly adopts the Universal Declaration of Human Rights on December 10, which was codrafted by Eleanor Roosevelt

1952   Eleanor resigns from the UN; soon after she becomes a volunteer at the American Association for the United Nations

1957   Meets Soviet leader Nikita Khrushchev

1960   Meets with future president John F. Kennedy, urging him to appoint more women to government positions of power

1962   Dies of tuberculosis on November 7

Index

Jane Anderson Vercelli, a summa cum laude graduate of the University of Hartford with a degree in philosophy, has been a news reporter for the *Associated Press* based in Washington, D.C., and a teacher of English and journalism. She is the author of *Inn Perspective: A Guide to New England Inns* and lives in Thompson, Connecticut, with her husband, architect Peter J. B. Vercelli, and their two sons.

Picture Credits